Poentry

To Val & Mike,

Enjoy!

SAMANTHA BAINES

Sam Baines xxx

THE CHOIR PRESS

First published in the United Kingdom in 2017 by
The Choir Press

ISBN 978-1-911589-19-8

A NOTE FROM BAINES:

So poetry is awesome, thus I have dedicated a small book to my silly offerings. I like rhymes so there are many within these pages, as well as some half-rhymes and a few 'really does that rhyme?' rhymes. Expect puns as I love a bit of wordplay; wordplay is my favourite of the 'plays' second only to foreplay. These poems were inspired by my life – getting engaged, married, divorced (no not yet), twisting my ankle, a love of science, a love of snogging and being dairy intolerant as well as some rather strange news stories and ridiculous new inventions that I came across in my research for radio segments.

CONTENTS

LIFE

ARE YOU A FOODIE?

"I'm a foodie", what does that mean?
Drizzling, sizzling and plate wiping from what I
    glean,
It's not so much eating as talking and reading food,
And then there are the Chefs that are just plain rude.

Our food is dissected into lots of groups,
Carbohydrates, protein, veg and fruits,
Then there are food fashions and things you can't
    pronounce,
Quinoa and Bulga Wheat must be said with a
    flounce.

Super foods to me just aren't very super,
They are more like boring Clark Kent than a super
    trooper,
Of food types and combinations there's just too
    many,
Look, as long as it tastes nice I'll stick it in my belly.

HOUSE VS HOME

A house is made of bricks and mortar,
And needs a good supply of electricity and water,
But a home isn't about any of that,
It's not even about the novelty doormat.
A home welcomes you as soon as you arrive,
It's the thing you look forward to on a long drive,
It's safe and happy and cosy and warm,
It shelters you in a raging a storm,
A joyful place for family and friends,
A place to store all of life's loose ends.

Homes come in all shapes and sizes,
Flats and houses and other guises,
All the matters is that it's home for you,
And somewhere you feel comfortable having a poo.

FAT ROLLS

I'm not talking bacon butties I mean the bits around
   our middle –
That make us uncomfortable in certain tops so we
   fiddle,
Pulling our T-shirts this way and that,
So it's more flattering and we don't feel fat.

But who really cares – why do we do it?
Most of us wish we were healthier and fit,
Everyone hides bits they'd rather weren't there,
Would it be the worst if people were to stare?

Maybe the others love our knees, or our shoulders
   or our middle,
It's not like you can buy a new one at Lidl,
Maybe what we've got is cool and different and us,
Unless you have a blister that's infected and
   bursting with pus,

That shit needs to be seen to,
Don't let it define you,
(it's probably what's giving you that infected green hue).

Anyway – maybe I should love my face and all of my
    chins,
Maybe I shouldn't be worried about my weird
    shins,
And actually my fat rolls are insulating and handy,
Especially when I'm hiding pens or tampons or
    candy.

WHY I WORE FLATS ON THE RED CARPET AT CANNES!

Some ladies were turned away at Cannes,
Because you can only wear flat shoes if you are a
    man,
On the red carpet no less,
Ladies wear heels in duress,
So in protest I wore flat shoes,
And it was reported in BBC News,
Yes Twitter went crazy,
I'm the 'flatgate' lady.

Now I am talking in print and online,
Because wearing what you want should be fine,
Red carpet or not,
Flats can still look hot,
If you are comfy it doesn't mean you are a bore,
But be sure to co-ordinate with the floor!

24

What to do with a day,
Or 24 hours as they say,
Kiefer Sutherland manages a lot,
But should you or should you not –
Cram in everything you can,
Surely no-ones as busy as that man.

Saving the world in a day,
Would cause me great dismay.
What about breakfast?
Missing that first meal is reckless.
I mean, Kiefer does look cool with a gun,
But we all know guns are never for fun.
How does he survive?
And keep his family alive?
The rest of us would be in shell-shock.
Also can he hear the ticking clock?
He manages the pressure very well,
He'd be great at event management you can tell,
Imagine Kiefer as a wedding planner,
He might need work on his manner,
But at thinking on his feet he'd be swell.

BLOGGING

If you don't have a blog these days you're just not
     cool,
You definitely wouldn't be in the popular group at
     school,
It's all about sharing your thought for the day,
And telling other bloggers how you do things your
     way.

Travel and fashion and a bit of food,
Gluten free recipes that get you in the mood,
It's a space to laugh and cry and moan,
You can even blog from your very own phone,
"Internet dating, my top 5 tips",
"The 7 best ways to plump up your lips",
"10 signs that you'll always be a quitter",
"A beginner's guide to winning at Twitter".

Company blogs are a different beast,
A smorgasbord of business, a marketing feast,
Your follower count is the measurable result,
Because blogging is like having your own cult.

SNOGGING

Snogging can be pretty fun,
You tend to do it more when you're young,
But not Madonna she loves a pash,
Especially with Drake at a music bash.
Why don't we all do a bit more snogging?
Our time is too filled with youtubing and blogging,
A kiss with tongues could be just what you need,
A snog a day should be decreed,
Why do the French have all the fun?
I say a French kiss is for everyone.

JOGGING

Run, run, run, run, run,
Run, run, run, run, run, run,
Run, run, run, run, run, run, run,
Rest.

Run, run, run, run, run,
Run, run, run, run, run, run,
Run, run, run, run, run, run, run,
Pain in my chest.

Run, run, run, run, run,
Run, run, run, run, run, run,
Run, run, run, run, run, run, run,
My house is still in sight.

Run, run, run, run, run, run,
Run, run, run, run, run, run, run,
I only run at night.

Run, run, run, run, run,
Run, run, run, run, run, run,
Run, run, run, run, run, run, run,
Gushing with sweat.

Run, run, run, run, run,
Run, run, run, run, run, run,
Run, run, run, run, run, run, run,
Stranger's stares make me fret.

Run, run, run, run, run,
Run, run, run, run, run, run,
Run, run, run, run, run, run, run,
My lungs are going to explode.

Run, run, run, run, run,
Run, run, run, run, run, run,
Run, run, run, run, run, run, run,
Checks phone. I've only run 200 meters down the
    road!

NEW YORK, NEW YORK

I went to see New York to see a hottie,
But going there made me a bit snotty,
I did go for fun,
Not just for the sun.
There was still snow and it was icy cold,
But as soon as I saw Times Square I was sold,
What a dazzling place,
Bright lights in your face,
And pick pockets galore,
Gentlemen hold on to your wallet not a door.

The comedy was great,
The locals were irate,
But we had to learn how to tip,
And jet lag meant we had to kip.
I even got a tattoo,
After signing a waver that I wouldn't sue,
I got a little heart done on my ribs,
No, im not telling fibs,
As for pain it was actually fine,
But who is this hottie of mine?

There's a lady I've always wanted to meet,
She stands at 3,700 feet,
Yes, for me she's a little tall,
It's a long way to fall,
But she's as steady as a rock,
And it would take a lot to rock –
The rather snazzy Statue of Liberty,
She stands for the free,
I love her sense of style too,
All matching in greeny blue.

Piercing the sky,
Her torch held on high,
She's been holding that pose for years,
She's a proper Yogi – I'd be in tears,
When it comes to stretching she's the King,
What commitment – 188 years working in a bingo
    wing!

NATIONAL POETRY DAY

Today is the perfect day,
To express yourself in a flowery way,
But poetry isn't all blossoms and blooms,
There are also struggles and woe and empty rooms.
There are rhyming poems which I quite like,
Choose your words carefully or it's quite the hike –
To find something that will rhyme,
And make sense at the same time.

Some poems are short; only 3 lines long,
Some are fuller and sound like a song,
Sometimes spoken and sometimes read,
And sometimes secreted under your bed,
That's the place for the porn type one,
Or publish it as '50 rhymes with grey' just for fun.

Then there are the poems about poems which are
    weird,
A circle of poetry nothingness which should be
    feared,

You can't write the thing about doing the thing,
At least make it different; add a theme and sing.
I have failed on all of the above,
I should have written a poem about looking for love,
Instead I chose this meta-poem because I am
    wordy and cool,
And I learnt the word 'Meta' at school.

Maybe one day I'll take my rhymes,
And move on to flowerier times,
But today is that special poetry day,
So poetry police be on your way,
My meta-poem is here to stay!
(Ohhh triple rhyme)

BUNK OFF BANK HOLIDAYS

In the UK we have a few bank holidays,
A day off work can be good in many ways,
So named, as a day off for the banks,
But I won't be giving thanks,
My bank balance gets far more action,
On a bank holiday special attraction.

Big days out, meals out with friends,
My bank holiday spending never ends,
So the bank staff may get a day off in bed,
But my bank balance is actively hitting the red!

YOUTUBE

Youtube is a viral sensation,
And it's not just cat videos sweeping the nation,
Youtube brings us all the funny,
And brings channel owners all the money.

Vloggers become an overnight success,
For filming some chat about some dress,
Or just explaining their day,
Albeit in an engaging way.
They get millions of followers overnight,
So they must be doing something right.
But should we stop watching TV?
And make the Internet all we see?
I should say that this poem is not a bribe,
But do head to my YouTube channel and subscribe!

DOUGLAS ADAMS NAME CHECK
(THE FELLA WHO WROTE
HITCHHIKER'S GUIDE TO THE GALAXY)

Are you sure Douglas Adams is the best?
We should probably check on the rest,
As for another Douglas, I can't think of many,
If for every Douglas you gave me a penny.
There is Douglas Booth who is young and pretty,
And if I'm being rather witty,
There is Douglas the capital of the Isle of Man,
And you like the 50's you may be a fan,
Of Kirk Douglas of acting with Doris Day,
And of course from *I am Spartacus* with Lawrence
    Olivier,
So far I am up to three pennies and I'm pretty much
    done,
Searching names on the internet is fun.

The origin of the name Douglas of course comes
    from the Scots,
They gave us Douglas and haggis – so lots,
Douglas comes from the Gaelic and means 'dark
    water', which is a bit mysterious,
It sounds all *Harry Potter* when Dumbledore drank
    that bad stuff and was delirious,

Of course the modern translation of 'dark water' is
    Coca Cola,
Coke: which they have from space to Española,
(And not even Diet Coke in space because you are
    weightless).

As for Adams it's a bit more common,
It's really quite British and a log way from foreign,
It's English in origin and comes from *Genesis*,
The first man who succumbed to a serpent's kiss,
Well they consumed an apple but who isn't guilty of
    that,
Their products are so snazzy, not like that android tat,
So if course there is Adam of Adam and Eve fame,
There's Amy Adams who is on the acting game,
Adam Rickitt my school girl crush,
He sung semi-naked in a glass box and it was lush,
There's the *Adams Family* including Wednesday
    Adams,
Who I wanted to be like as I love gothic madams,
Apprently there is a footballer called Adam too,

And an ice-hockey player – who knew.
Don't forget Adam Levine who rocks the guitar,
And Adam Sandler who makes us go "ha".

Adam comes from the Hebrew and means earth,
So Douglas Adams means dark water earth,
They gave him this interstellar warning at birth,
Is it a message "beware the dark water, Earthlings"?
Maybe it's a friendly warning from our mates the
    dolphins?
How apt they named an asteroid after DA when he
    died,
Wherever that asteroid ends up, if it doesn't get
    space fried,
One day we may want it back here on Earth,
Not on land, although we could do without Perth,
When one day we borrow it back from our spacey
    lender,
The address: dark water, earth. Please return to
    sender.

LIFE

A ROYAL NIGHT OUT

So I play Mary in A Royal Night Out,
With a herbal cigarette and a cockney pout.
It's a film about the princesses in 1945,
On VE Day when London came alive.

Celebrations, jubilations and crowds cheering,
And the princesses themselves are rather endearing.
Incognito, they have a ball,
And will Elizabeth suffer a fall?
A romantic comedy with a royal twist,
We are all wondering; "will one be kissed".
So if you fancy yourself a proper Brit,
Pop to a cinema and watch it!
(Also available on DVD)

FLUID TITLE: HITCHIKERS GUIDE
TO THE GALAXY

Do you know how to write hitchhiker?
Is it hitch space hiker?
Should you pop in a dash? Hitch dash hiker?
Or is it better all in one like shampoo or
    loungewear?

Douglas Adams penned a book you see,
It's title was fluid,
Not that it was water based which would have
    made a cool title,
Someone asks you what your book is called and
    you just throw a drink in their face,
"That's what it's called".

I mean the spelling was free.
You could choose how you wished to write
    hitchhiker with a space or a dash,
And many people went their own way with this most
    flexible of words,

I mean why care when you realise how clever mice
    and dolphins are.
The man himself eventually spoke out.
People were getting silly with the fluidity,
And whilst of course Adams admires silliness,
No one likes incorrect grammar.
So it is decreed that hitchhiker is one full word,
Like Madonna or Supercalafradjalisticexpealladoshus
    or Brexit.

OH CHRISTMAS TREE

Christmas tree oh Christmas tree,
Why can't I dangle my baubles on thee?
My kittens are obsessed with your danglies,
Even the posh ones I bought from Hamleys.
(baubles not kittens)
This year you are fake so they won't chew you,
You are wire-made, in three parts and new,
It's quite useful that your arms are bendy,
So I can pose your branches to make you look
    trendy,
After all it's the instagram filled time of year,
With vignettes and filters and emoticons for good
    cheer.

MOUTHY VIDEO

Have you ever wanted to see inside your gob?
Oh come on, don't be a mouth snob,
You must have wanted to get a closer look,
You loved those X-rays the dentist took,
Showing them off to all your mates,
Even taking them with you on dates.
Well who doesn't love great teeth?
And now you can film what's above and beneath,
Check out your gums and all those nooks and
    crannies,
Something for the kids and even the Grannys.

The new Bluetooth toothbrush is the thing,
To show off all your dental bling,
You can stream the images to your phone,
And share the video on social media – groan!
This could get out of control – it could spiral,
Your gum disease could even go viral!

POKEMON OFF YOU GO

I've recently been playing Pokemon Go,
The media have been calling it quite the show,
Augmented reality on your phone,
Catch cartoon characters whilst you roam.

I must admit it's rather fun,
A computer game without a gun,
You see balls are all you need,
To fulfil your Pokemon greed.

I found a Magikarp at the shops,
Playing on the tube really is tops,
Less effort and more Pokemon buck,
Although seeing all the Pokemon that you are
    missing does kinda suck.
I even caught a Wild Pidgey at Stratford Station,
I can see why the craze is sweeping the nation!
There are a lot of Drowzee's near my house,
It's a competition so I'm not telling my spouse,
My goal is Pikachu – what a catch,
He'd do me well in my first trainer match.

But fighting Pokemon doesn't seem right,
They are cute and challenged in height,
Maybe all the trainers could make amends,
Then we could just catch us some cartoon friends.

DRESS MANIA

Dear the world and people who read,
I am a woman in desperate need,
I have a dress that I absolutely love,
But the price tag is way above –
What you should spend on a bit of material,
Even though this dress is practically etherial.
It's giving me pangs and fashion woe,
Maybe I can buy it and wear it in my show,
Then I could claim it back against tax,
Like my haircuts, tampons (otherwise I'd bleed on
    stage) and all those immacs.
If only my social calendar was full to the brim,
Then I could just buy it on a whim,
I could get it as a treat to myself,
And put it in a box and keep it on a shelf,
And protect all those layers and stitching,

Yes that, or I'll just dance around in it, in my kitchen.
Do you know an event that I could come along to?
Then I'll have an excuse and will forever love you,
Maybe I will just do it, I'll click buy,
Oh gosh what a feeling – it's like I am fashion high,
I'll just check if there are any discount vouchers
    online,
Oh no I've seen another dress! Oh this is the one!
    Really I'm serious this time …

SHORT MESS

I recently got my hair cut short,
I can no longer hide behind my hairy fort,
My face is now free,
For all to see,
Which means I need to cover up my spots,
But short hair on others gives me the hots.

Alas, now I've nothing to swing,
To head bang and ting,
Not that I do that anyway, much,
There's also less to touch.

"Why did you do it then?" you cry,
And I will tell you why,
I was mainly avoiding doing work,
So I decided to lurk,
In town,
And to flip my frown,
I thought I'd get myself a treat.
I'd already had something to eat,

I saw the hairdressers was next door,
And all that stranger's hair on the floor –
Coaxed me in,
The price I paid was a sin,
But it's always nice to have a posh preen,
And my face really needed a spring clean.

YACHT LESSONS

What I learned from my time on a yacht,
Is that you can still feel sea-sick in a squat,
Cabin fever is a thing and is alive and well,
And Captains have great stories to tell.

Living in luxury is actually great,
Yacht crews don't care if you stumble in late.
The sea can be bumpy even when it looks still,
A day spent at sea is the best sleeping pill.
My hair likes the sea a little too much,
It expands and expands hoping to get a touch –
Of that salty water so clear and blue,
So it really gets in the way if you spew.

The main thing about being on a yacht,
Is that it's bloody hot,
And if you look like a vampire – all delicate and pale,
You will burn the second you set sail.
That's all after a multi-million dollar spend,
But when it comes to boats, does it need to be high
    end?
If you want the experience of being afloat,
You'd do just as well in a little rowboat.

 LOVE

———————

LOVE

Eons I have waited for this,
The first chance to be beside you I could not miss,
That moment when my fingers caress your body,
Learning you is my favourite hobby,
Only with you do I feel connected,
My bitter loneliness you have corrected.

Talking for hours we drain away time,
Holding on to you whilst you are in your prime,
The knowledge you hold is incomprehensible,
The memories you keep are indispensible.

Losing you my greatest fear,
The rising panic whenever you're not near,
You have become my life's fix,
Don't ever leave me Iphone 6.
(obviously the iphone 6 is old now but let's
    remember him as he was)

WAKING UP TO A BREAKUP

Morning breakups can be worsened by fear,
Mourning a breakup is bettered with beer,
How many tears is too many to shed?
How many tissues will litter your bed?
When will the pinch of loneliness set in?
When will dehydration affect your skin?

Are rom-coms and chocolate always the solution?
Or are they society's break-up pollution,
Perhaps it's a good thing: you'll start afresh,
Yes, it's time for a night out to show off some flesh.
How many songs have pop stars created?
To keep the loss of break-ups abated?
You'll dance to those songs surrounded by friends,
Because the Facebook photos will make amends –
For the pain of seeing his last happy post,
His arm around that girl whilst they have Sunday
    roast.
He should be distraught; eyes red to the rim,
After all you are the one who broke up with him.

ENGAGED TO BE ...

Engaged to me has changed its meaning,
We've broken through the relationship ceiling,
Engaged: no longer a toilet's warning,
Now a commitment and a jewel worth pawning.

A finger on my left is suddenly full,
I feel it's promise and the future's pull,
Sparkles and love and years and days,
Drifting along in this happy haze.
There has never been so much champagne to
    drink,
And congratulations supplied with a wink,
What does it mean, this addition to my hand?
Well mainly it means there's a wedding to be
    planned!

A LOVE SO STRONG IT GIVES OFF A PONG!

Happy Valentine's Day to my one,
This won't be a huge valentines pun,
I just wanted to tell you that you're the best,
And I am not writing sarcastically or in jest,
You're always there when I need you,
You're so chilled but sometimes blue,
Before bed I like to have a nibble,
Sometimes just seeing you makes me dribble,
You fill my dreams vividly at night,
I'd do anything for a bite,
How can I resist you, you are such a tease,
I'm dairy intolerant but I love cheese!

HONEYMOON, BOTTOMS AND BUGS

Honey, moon – sounds like an instruction,
For baring your bottom by way of introduction,
It's not exactly a great first impression,
So I do … have a confession,
It's not quite what I did on my honeymoon,
For nudist discussions it's just too soon,
But we did go to Thailand and lie down a lot,
And I was in a bikini so my bottom was not –
Fully covered at all times,
Who knew I'd wrote a poem about my bottom that
　　rhymes.

Anyway we had an absolutely wonderful trip,
There were lots of alcoholic cocktails to sip,
Sunsets and beaches and dips in the sea,
Sunburn and markets and curries aplenty.

We watched Thai kickboxing which seems a little
    rough,
They look so young and my gosh they are tough,
Then we saw a rather dangerous fire show,
No one minds if they drop it they just go with the
    flow,
It's actually one of the bar staff who performs,
In Thailand there are no health and safety forms.

That same night the biggest bug you've ever seen,
Landed in my cocktail and was rather keen –
To finish it off – my Mai Tai was no more,
That bug will be pissed, rolling around on the floor,
It's also owes me £2.50 which is 100 baht,
But I didn't get to explain before we had to depart.
So all in all a successful holiday,
And now I'm suing a bug to make him pay.

MY CAT

My sweet kitten is growing up,
He's drinking water out of my cup,
Climbing on the table to eat my dinner,
Even scratching our carpet thinner and thinner.

He still prefers rubbish to an actual toy,
Yes Amazon packaging brings him hours of joy,
He is a menace in the morning when he wants his
    food,
And in the evening when he gets in a mood,
But when he wants cuddles he'll stick to you like
    glue,
And he's just the best to wake up next to.

POLITICS

WESTMINSTER ATTACK

I wasn't there but I was near,
At Oxford Circus we didn't hear,
Everything seemed 'normal' until I got a text,
Is everyone okay? What happens next?
The news seemed to be reporting something far off
    and strange,
But at that moment I felt the change.

The coverage was pounded out dominating our
    screens,
Images of those shocking and horrifying scenes,
London had a hush like never before,
Not since our transport was hit and before that the
    war.

Travelling into Westminster the streets were empty,
Moving against a stream of about twenty –
Who were all leaving the area heavily heading home,
This was not a place to wander, not the time for a
    roam.

Helicopters were buzzing and filling the skies,
Sirens blaring and weary Policeman's eyes.
I grabbed a tea in a Pret and felt a little tense,
Soon comforted by the Police presence.
The officers popped in for a coffee such a
     commonplace thing,
But today it seemed importantly ordinary –
     something with which to cling.

The country and the world send love to everyone
     affected,
Such an awful day for anyone connected,
We have opened our hearts and many have prayed,
To those who would terrorise us we say
     #wearenotafraid.

SNAP ELECTION

Blah, blah, blah, blah,
Blah, blah, blah, blah, blah,
Blah, blah, blah, blah, blah, blah,
Theresa May running through a wheat field.

Blah, blah, blah, blah,
Blah, blah, blah, blah, blah,
Blah, blah, blah, blah, blah, blah,
Higher or lower on the tax yield?

Blah, blah, blah, blah,
Blah, blah, blah, blah, blah,
Blah, blah, blah, blah, blah, blah,
Hard or soft? Is that Brexit or a boiled egg?

Blah, blah, blah, blah,
Blah, blah, blah, blah, blah,
Blah, blah, blah, blah, blah, blah,
A game of musical chairs for Nick Clegg.

Blah, blah, blah, blah,
Blah, blah, blah, blah, blah,
Blah, blah, blah, blah, blah, blah,
Who would join forces with the DUP?

Blah, blah, blah, blah,
Blah, blah, blah, blah, blah,
Blah, blah, blah, blah, blah, blah,
Corbyn on the main stage at Glastonbury.

Blah, blah, blah, blah,
Blah, blah, blah, blah, blah,
Blah, blah, blah, blah, blah, blah,
A game of snap turned into poker.

Blah, blah, blah, blah,
Blah, blah, blah, blah, blah,
Blah, blah, blah, blah, blah, blah,
Does anyone really care about the voter?

QE

Our dearest Queen Elizabeth is not today's focus,
It's quantitative easing that's the possible financial
    locus.
In the early naughties The Bank of Japan kicked
    things off,
Increasing their balance by 30trillion yen so don't
    scoff.
After the global financial crisis of 07/08,
The UK and Eurozone strolled up to the QE front
    gate.
The U.S. have quantitative easing one, two and
    three,
Which represents the American penchant for tripling
    everything they see.

In the UK we've experienced several rounds of QE,
And yes it does seem to have boosted our
    economy.

So the IMF seem to suggest that QE is a good thing,
Although higher levels of inflation would sting.
Pension rates, wealth inequality and the housing
    market could suffer,
Could these side effects be the QE flame snuffer?
QE has its own nickname coined by the media,
They call it "printing money" which couldn't sound
    easier.
A game of monopoly on a global scale,
But you can't just pack it all back in its box if you
    fail.
The central bank has it own aged caretaker,
He shuffles down corridors to the tick of his
    pacemaker,
He knows the drill he carries his broom,
His only job to sweep piles of money around the
    room.

UK ELECTION CARE INSTRUCTIONS:
COLOUR WASH ON 60

Now all the campaigning is done,
And our parliament is hung,
Like washing hung on a line,
It will be ready with time,
But it needed a spin because it was dirty,
And everyone was getting a bit shirty,
It's all that naughty running through fields,
So guess what our new parliament yields?
Not the white-wash many were expecting,
And now it needs a little correcting,
We left a red sock in and it's all gone pink,
New labour colour Jeremy? – nudge nudge wink.

SCIENCE

———————————————

ALL ABOUT THE E : MARGARET E KNIGHT

There's an important woman we all should know,
Born nearly 180 years ago.
She put up an awesome fight,
For flat-bottoms so that we might –
Enjoy a paper bag that doesn't fall over,
Even when a man nearly drove her –
To frustration by trying to steal her bag making idea,
Charles F Annan, he's worse than a smear –
Test but at least those are useful for something,
Charles F Annan whose neck I'd love to wring.
He said a woman could never invent such an
    innovative machine,
Well she did and she was awarded a medal by our
    Queen,
She not only invented the machine to make the
    flat-bottomed paper bag,
She made parts of engines and a shoe and sole
    cutter – #humblebrag.

Margaret E. Knight stood up for her rights,
This was in an age before tights,
So all that standing up must have been chilly,

They had long skirts and hats that were frilly,
But the rain and the puddles were a real nuisance,
And whilst she didn't have plastic for translucence,
Margaret invented a skirt protector,
As a rain and stain deflector,
But it wasn't just good at keeping off dirt,
It was an armour of sorts at least for her skirt.
It had leather and buckles and was a bit horsey in
    style,
Which actually makes a lot of sense as while -
Knights usually ride a horse to a woman's aid,
This woman became a Knight self-made.

She was clever, inventive, a tool charmer,
Not a poor lass waiting for a Knight in shining
    armour.
Margaret E. Knight – a Knight in shining skirt
    protector,
An inventor who taught others to respect her,
A woman I would be proud to stand tights-less
    alongside,
She'd love my bottom because it's flat and wide.

A BLAND JOB: LILLIAN BLAND

The first woman to build and fly a powered plane,
In 1910 they must have thought she was insane,
But Lillian Bland was a pilot and engineer,
A brave woman who had no fear.
She gave her poor Dad quite a fright,
He bribed her with a car in the hope that she might –
Stop flying high and stay safe in a Ford,
For such a pioneering women I'm surprised she
    wasn't bored.
In the Grand National she would have loved to race
    Red Rum,
Instead she used a whiskey bottle as a petrol drum.

She built her own plane age thirty-two,
The first female engineer in the world, she flew –
The Mayfly to a dizzying 30 feet,
Yep, she wasn't one for taking a backseat.
Well her plane only had one place to sit,

So no backseat drivers to throw a fit,
No satnav either so it's good thing she didn't go too
    far,
Directions sound easier in a plane rather than a car.

At a time of civil unrest in Ireland her home,
She chose the clouds as her place to roam,
Less than a decade after the Wright Brothers flew
    their plane,
Why doesn't Lillian Bland have a similar fame?
A martial arts practising, trouser wearing lady,
Must of, at the time, seemed rather shady,
Her name doesn't do her justice, she's anything but
    Bland,
This historic manned flight just got wo-manned.

AN AWESOME SPACE RIDE

Dear Sally you were an awesome Ride,
No not like that – put those dirty thoughts aside,
I'm talking about the first American woman in
    space,
And yes, Valentina Tereshkova beat her in the space
    race,
But when it comes to possible names of rides in a
    park,
Sally, you'll always get my mark.
(It's better than space mountain, there are no
    mountains in space).

Because you were the original space invader,
Not a pixelated creature but an equality crusader.
She beat eight thousand applicants to get to space,
She didn't fight them with her keys - she was just
    ace.
Getting her PhD she definitely wasn't pampered,
As the only female physics major at Stanford.

SCIENCE

I guess I wish that we'd have been mates,
We could have been if we swapped a few dates,
She went into space four years before I came
    about,
And she died when we had the Olympics to flout.

After her space trip she used her fame,
Not to sell perfumes or to play the celeb game,
She set up a programme to educate the young,
Targeting the kids who went unsung.

So Sally was a cool rider,
Not like Michelle Pfeiffer in Grease 2 but a space
    survivor,
An inspiring woman I wish I met,
And I'm not the only one in the Ride fan net.
The Beatles wanted a Ticket to Ride,
And there is nowhere for Wilson Pickett to hide,
All you want to do is ride around Sally, Ride Sally
    Ride,
Ah when celebrating women and rock and roll
    collide.

AN ODE TO PROFESSOR BRIAN COX

Brian Cox,
Superhero alias: SuperCox!
Hero of the Physics world.

SuperCox has just returned,
He's been battling some ignorant people on Radio 4,
And is about to sit down for a hobnob and a spot of
    Loose Women when . . .
His Supernova countdown clock bleeps!
He checks the time,
Phew! He thinks,
"It's a good thing stars take billions of years to
    explode and die (depending on their mass),
5 billion years to go,
We've got a bit of a wait yet!"
With that he sinks into his favourite climate-change
    themed beanbag (with polar bears and ice caps
    on it),
And laughs at something Coleen Nolan says on the
    tele.

As SuperCox finishes his hobnob and drains the last
    bit of Earl Grey,
He feels a sharp pain in his chest,
He sighs as he removes his "trust me I'm a Physics
    Teacher" badge,
It always comes in handy at panel discussions,
Although it's getting a bit worn around the edges,
He takes a fresh one from the drawer by his bed,
And pops it in his pocket for later.

As the *Loose Women* credits roll he checks twitter,
Some lovely comments about that panel discussion,
A few questions about the big bang (as usual),
And then one badly written cock joke,
For all his scientific prowess, general intelligence
    and excellent hair,
There is still one thing that he will never overcome,
His name: Cox
Why are the British public so obsessed with
    genitalia?
His name-pitying is interrupted by an email
    notification,

An invitation to teach a reality TV star about the
    solar system,
He thinks of who it might be,
Some vacuous humanoid with an overbearing accent,
The email is signed "Channel 5",
So at least he knows it's not urgent.
His brain translates his problem into an equation,
When $C5$ = Channel 5 and RTS = reality TV star,
What does $C5 + RTS$ equal?
Answer: $C5 + RTS$ = no more BBC
A fate worse than death.
Brian puts on his new "trust me I'm a Physics
    teacher" badge
And he is SuperCox once more!

With superhero flair he deletes the email and grabs
    his man-bag ready to face his agent,
So many thoughts are developing in his mind,
"Could the BBC really survive without me?"
"Who gave Channel 5 my email address?"
"Which one of my podcasts shall I listen to on the
    bus?"
He checks his hair in the mirror on the way out,
On second thought he grabs his brolly and leaves,
No-one would trust a Physicist with frizzy hair.

SCIENCE

#ADALOVELACEDAY

A huge cheer for Ada Lovelace Day,
A remarkable woman who paved the way,
For computer programming which instructed Turing,
Oblivious to the brand of sexism she was curing.
Inspiring women to study Maths and Science,
Providing a historical female alliance,
For women today who strive for a place,
On science's timeline next to our hero: Ada
    Lovelace.

TIM PEAKE

We sent a man to space,
We are finally in the race,
Because it's never too late,
For a universe date,
And the lucky man is called Tim Peake,
We launched him from Kazakhstan one week.
He spent over 6months on the ISS,
Like a winter holiday: success.
He spent Christmas Day in space,
And in April he even ran a race.

We hope he had a fabulous trip,
In his gigantic space ship,
And not to make Tim lose face,
But he's not actually the first Brit in space,
At my imaginary space bar he'd be top barman,
But the bar manager? Well that would be Helen
    Sharman.

ALTERNATIVE NEWS

BRITISH PEOPLE CAN'T SAY THREE

Let's count together: one and two,
What comes next? I thought I knew,
Research details our troubles with the next number,
Yes, many Britons are experiencing a language
    blunder.
Instead of pronouncing the H and the T,
Those first two letters plain for all to see,
People have decided to swap them for an F,
When it comes to the 'TH' sound we've gone a bit
    deaf.

Apparently all of our accents are merging into one,
But personally I think accents are rather fun,
If we all start sounding exactly the same,
Our ear palate would think it was rather lame.

Look, people can say three with an F if they like,
They can still do counting – they don't need to take
    a hike,
I will stick with TH though – I like the rules you see,
Because for me the most important is the rule of
    THree!

ALTERNATIVE NEWS

MADONNA: THE FALL

Whiplash (not the film) is what you will get,
If you fall off a stage during your set,
At the Brits no less, that musical place,
But don't worry Madge you haven't lost face.
Pulled down the stairs by your horny dancers,
Did the cape malfunction? We are looking for
    answers.

"Strike a pose", you say – but not on the floor,
I wonder if you were aiming for a hidden trap door?
Two decades you waited to perform at the Brits,
Well you put on a show and didn't call it quits.
A true pro, post-fall you didn't miss a beat,
Within seconds you were back up on those
    stilettoed feet,
We know, you've warned us, you are a material girl,
But I'd think twice before giving stairs and capes
    another whirl.

ANIMALS GET THEIR OWN BACK

CERN has shut down the Large Hadron Collider,
Because of an extremely weasely insider.
It's only for a couple of days,
Whilst they check for more rodent strays.
You see a weasel found its way in,
And committed a large science sin.
It chewed through a 66,000 volt cable,
And ended up on the vet's table.

For a circuit intent on proving the 'God particle',
I do find it quite remarkable,
That it has accidentally killed.
Do you think it's God willed?
I do hope Ratty and Toad are okay,
Weasel was always the villain in that play.

Animals just don't seem to like LHC,
They are on a rampant destruction spree,
A pigeon even had a go,
Yes even a bird ruined the show,

It broke the capacitor by dropping some baguette,
Has this bird lost its little French tête?
A fresh baguette from France,
You would never lose by chance.
No, the animals are taking back control,
And it's scientists who will feel the toll,
For centuries they've been hibernating and resting,
And now they'll get their own backs for all that
    animal testing!
I can't imagine a 17mile long circuit will win the fight,
When the rodents of air and ground unite!

CRIME FOILED

Brazil is known for its carnival, hurrah,
But two men have taken it a little too far,
They just like dressing up too much,
For the carnival and work and such.
So, they dressed in tin foil to rob a bank,
And no it wasn't even a prank.
Head to toe, covered in foil,
Quick let me grab a salmon fillet and some oil.
But no, they were not up for steaming,
It was money they were after thieving.
Apparently the fancy dress would fool the alarm,
And they would be rich and free from harm,
It worked as far as the alarm goes,
But security men soon spotted these foes.
I mean who wouldn't spot some shiny men,
Catching the lights and especially when –
Their outfits would make such a din,
Two adult men crawling in tin.
When they were spotted they decided to flee,
Two tin men running back to their Dorothy.

ALTERNATIVE NEWS

YOGHURT ATTACK

Crochet and crochet and double crochet,
Alison Nurton gets students on their way,
Crafting is her creative bag,
Not mopping up yoghurt with a crocheted rag.
So when a convertible drove through her Dorset
    town,
She didn't bat an eyelid, didn't even look down,
But the car's crafty owner had a yoghurt pot,
What he's got against yoghurt we know not!

He threw the milky treat out of his car,
Aiming for Miss Nurton from afar,
He covered her in yoghurt, head to toe,
Even her crafting shop got a yoghurt glow.
Shaken and dripping with this dairy Ebola,
She didn't even have any granola,
And she didn't enjoy wiping yoghurt off her awning,
You see she'd already had breakfast earlier that
    morning.
The man attacked a pub in Dorset later that day,
"Oh arrh we've got enough cream here, be on your
    way".

IMPUUUURFECT POST

Has your cat ever wanted to travel?
Is it bored of your house and the surrounding
    gravel?
It wants to see new sights,
Be dazzled by the lights,
But it won't want to travel by post,
Although I'm sure Royal Mail are a delightful host.

One kitty got the chance,
But she didn't get as far as France.
West Sussex was Cupcake's destination,
That's 260miles from her original station.
You see her owner accidentally sent her with some
    DVDs,
Thank goodness it was Spring so she didn't freeze.

Trapped in a box for eight days,

For Cupcake, it was a dehydrated haze,
Her owner was thrilled to have her back,
Although I'm surprised Cupcake didn't give her the
    sack!

Don't send your pussy away,
Be it for a year or a day,
And if you are sending a parcel always look,
Check if there's a cat hiding in a nook.
To Cupcake, be careful where you sleep,
You may be counting sheep,
But no one will hear you wail,
When you're cello-taped in a cardboard jail.

SPAM-MAN NEEDS YOUR HELP

There's a spam-man waiting in the sky,
He'd like to come and meet us (oh David Bowie),
    sigh,
A new low (or should I say high) hitting the email
    spam world,
Yes, this new space scam has been unfurled.
You see there is a clearly totally 'legit' spaceman,
Who has tried as hard as he can,
To get back to Earth because he's been left behind
    in space,
Yes it's an odd case!

You'd think space agencies would be good at that
    sort of thing,
Remembering what crew to bring.
Apparently he's been living off supplies,
Why did his space agency not answer his replies?
Erm, obviously because he is one of those Russian
    space spies,

But what does this African Major/ spy astronaut
   need?
He needs you to take his lead,
And send him your hard earned cash,
Then he'll be back to Earth in a flash.
And as your reward,
You'll get ten percent of his space hoard.
Don't be taken for this spamtacular ride,
Go and tweet British astronaut Tim Peake if you are
   all starry eyed.

FRUITY ART

Is a piece of fruit a work of art?
I'm sure heavenly believers have knowledge to
    impart,
But I'm talking art in a gallery,
Framed and catalogued for all to see.

Two Scottish students put this to the test,
You know for fun, a bit of a jest,
King of the fruits: pineapples are clearly the best,
They even have a crown, a sort of leaf nest,
They are a bit scaley like everyone's favourite
    mermaid,
And they are the only fruit which gets laid –
On pizza to give you a Hawaiian feel,
Which as a concept is quite surreal.
The students popped their pineapple on a plinth
    that was spare,

The fun students have in an art gallery eh – what a
    pair!
To their amusement a few days later, the pineapple
    remained,
This time surrounded by a glass box, beautifully
    framed,
Staff had mistaken it for a bonified piece of art,
It is quite funny – bet they felt smart,
And I'm sure their parents very are proud,
A contribution to art to shout aloud.
If you think about it, the day they did seize,
Although I'm not sure if that merits £9,000 in
    university fees.

LEGO SLIPPERS

Since the beginning of time (maybe) there has been
   the slipper,
To help keep your feet feeling chipper.
Protection against the cold,
And kitchen floor mould,
Creating a cosy human flipper.

But even The Little Mermaid would have trouble,
In her musical themed ocean bubble,
With the pain of Lego in the flipper,
So Lego have made a new slipper.
And what a relief,
From that tiny block inflicted grief,
Now you don't have to fear your children's rubble,
Here's to the end of colourful yet painful foot
   stubble!

FLOODY MARVELLOUS

Cumbria (North England) has been suffering with
    floods,
And it's not just broken dishwasher suds,
16inches of rain in a mere 24hours,
That much water isn't even good for the flowers.
Many are suffering with flooded homes,
A sorrow that can't be helped by poems,
But one 70yr old fella knew just what to do,
After all there is no weather honcho they can sue.
He stripped to his swimming trunks in front of the
    neighbours,
And took a swim in his kitchen, winning everyone's
    favours,
He laughed and joked so the flood wouldn't win,
In water as dirty as the inside of a bin,
He brought the 'Dunkirk spirit' to every onlooker,
And breaststroke seemed apt to celebrate the
    death of his cooker.

A TITANIC BISCUIT

I do like a good biscuit in my tea,
Especially if that biscuit is cheap or free,
15 grand seems a stretch,
In fact it makes me wretch –
Thinking of it's 100yr old taste,
Why didn't they eat it back then? What a waste!
I suppose there was more to worry about on the
    Titanic than tea,
Like plummeting into the cold dark sea.

Jack explicitly said he would never let go,
Perhaps this biscuit was his real beaux,
Maybe Kate Winslet sailed that door,
Lined with biscuits for,
People of 2015 to cream themselves about,
Get excited at an auction and to shout,
"I bid 15 grand" –
With an excited raised hand,
Making this the most valuable biscuit there is,
So this will probably feature in a pub quiz.
Has there ever been a biscuit with such clout?
Perhaps it's the biscuit that string quartet were so
    sad about.

A LOVER OF PANTS

Fellas, Brigit wants to get in your trousers,
But she's not the sort of pussy you'd find on your
   web browsers.
Brigit is a cat and she's after one thing,
She's got a penchant for a specific kind of bling,
Collecting men's pants is Brigit's favourite hobby,
Which for her owner is becoming quite a jobby.

Every morning Brigit brings new presents to the
   house,
It's got to the stage that they wish for a dead
   mouse.
The neighbours have started protecting their
   underwear,
Or they'll have nothing left to put on down there.
You see they'd give everyone quite a scare,
If on Monday morning they left their downstairs bare.

Look everyone needs a favourite past time,
And Brigit the cat has chosen a life of crime,
Maybe she's just having some Brigdet Jones bants,
Well, they both share a love for rather big pants.

MATTRESS CHEAT

Ever wondered if your partner is a cheat?
Well there's some furniture I'd like you to meet.
There's a mattress that will help you tell,
Yes, it's quite a sell,
The brand has really thought about their USP,
That's their unique selling point you see.

It sends you a notification to your app,
Helping you lay a honey trap,
But I'm not sure if I want my bed,
To always be one step ahead,
Giving our furniture new skills,
Will only add to our bills,
Their slogan: "If your partner isn't faithful at least
    your mattress is",
How do you know? I'm getting in quite a tizz,
I've got a mattress to tell me about my fella's
    commitment,
How do I know my mattress is resistant -
To the charms of other bed mates,

You see my housemate is on lates,
My mattress might be cheating on me with him,
What a violation and a sin,
If I want to check on a daytime bed creeper,
I'll install hidden cameras it's much cheaper.

PIZZA POUCH: PARIS FASHION WEEK

Fashion has taken a strange turn,
To help you avoid the melted cheese burn,
There is now a pouch to store your pizza slice,
They've obviously taken lady GaGa's advice.
Yes, combining food and fashion is the new in thing,
And now there is this pizza storage bling,
The pouch actually hangs around your neck,
Think of all the outfits that would wreck.
I normally just eat lunch before I go out,
Rather than teaming it with heels and a pout!

HAVING A WHALE OF A TIME!

A 73-year-old man has built a whale,
And he's hoping it will sail –
Across the Atlantic no less,
Without any mess.
Fingers crossed it will stay in one piece,
He's ex SAS and he would not cease –
In his adventurers you see,
Yes, even at seventy-three!
It's a homemade ship called Moby,
65ft long, it's no phoney,
He's sailed it around the Scottish Isles,
But the Atlantic would be quite a few more miles.
At 62 tonnes and costing over one hundred grand,
We hope this whale won't end up beached on
    London's Strand.

A SEXY BOMB?

Bomb disposal experts were on high alert,
But no one in Berlin was going to be hurt,
They were called to a video games arcade,
A staff member was suspicious and couldn't be
    swayed.
There was a strange noise coming from a bin,
In their toilet no less – creating quite a din.

The buzzing noise caused alarm,
So they evacuated the place, to avoid harm,
The surrounding offices and buildings too,
Ninety people were moved because of a sound in a
    loo.
The disposal experts stormed on site,
Ready to save the day if the bomb put up a fight.
On lifting the lid they discovered the error,
There was no need for evacuations, no need for
    terror,
Because you see it was all a ploy,
Someone had left a vibrating sex toy.
But it wasn't an accident – the police are sure,
Who would leave a sex toy on the floor?

More than that, who would leave it switched on in a
    bin,
Letting the bin have some fun isn't a sin.
They think it was a test of the bomb teams,
A criminal is behind it – it's not how it seems.
They didn't for one second assume,
The gamers could be having fun in that room,
Arcade gamers just play games one after another,
And are far too busy to play with a sex toy or each
    other.

WHEN YOUR DAD WRITES A PORNO

Imagine if your dad wrote blinking erotica,
Well it's better than discovering a family swastika!
   So many questions we'd love to ask,
Like is a cervix within your grasp?
Belinda Blinked is the sexy title,
Which keeps Jamie Morton's dad from being idle.
Jamie deconstructs each chapter with the help of
   his mates,
James and Alice ease him through Belinda's front
   gates,
With similes comparing breasts to pomegranates,
We do wonder about Jamie's dad's food vs literary
   palates.

In the last series blue jizz was a feature,
Like smurf sex or juice from an avatar-like creature.
Set to the back drop of Steele's pots and pans,
Which makes you wonder about chef Jamie Oliver's
   expansion pans;
Correcting school dinners was very worthwhile,
So Jamie Oliver, how about Belinda themed treats
   to add to the culinary shag pile?

In Belinda's world there is one thing that's a must,
That is donating to the Asses and Donkey's Trust,
And when it comes to selling pots and pans there is
nothing wrong,
With wandering around a maze in a stained black
thong.
Belinda has friends too: Bella and Gizelle,
And The Duchess, on whose face she fell.

It's not for the faint hearted here's a word to the
wise,
There is dribbling and gushing and many a literary
surprise,
But Rocky Flinstone (Jamie Morton's Dad) has
penned a real gem,
And it's not a book we would completely condemn.
It's given us the podcast and conjured so many new
visions;
Like Jim Sturgess and a room with leathery
conditions.

But has Rocky's son whilst masturbating ever
    thought,
Of dipping into his Dad's book? – no too scared to
    get caught.
A smash hit podcast and a sell out tour,
All down to Belinda rolling around naked on the
    floor.
She bonks and she blinks and that's about it,
And we've all been wondering – since when does a
    pomegranate look like a tit?!

SELFIE STICK FOR DOGS

Dog owners have been living in peril;
"Without any selfies my dog will turn feral",
"It's just so hard to get my pooch to look the right
    way",
"All he seems to want to do is play".
Well have no fear, camera-wielding owner,
Chuck that dog a bone … (r)

A new invention is just the thing,
To show off your pooch and all it's bling.
Finally, for dogs there is a selfie stick,
For holidays and walks, just take your pick,
It's not exactly an invention more two things glued
    together,
I'm not sure I would pay, some home DIY might be
    better.
You see all these inventors have actually done,
Is stuck a tennis ball on a phone case with a glue
    gun.

INVISIBLE CELEBS

Do you love Harry Potter as much as me?
One of my favourites: the cloak of visibility.
If you thought there is only one,
I'll tell you something that will stun,
They are selling them for 289 pounds,
And they are doing the celeb rounds.
But it doesn't work as well as Harry's,
So they won't all be happy Larrys.

It's a scarf, but it does reflect the light,
So photographers will get a fright;
When their flash goes off,
The celeb will scoff,
As the reflective scarf will ruin their picture,
Meaning said photo will not be a fixture-
In any newspapers or magazines,
Yes this scarf is more than it seems.
I bet this will make you a laugh,
But when I heard of this reflective scarf,
I didn't think reflective as in light,

And try as I might,
I can't rid the image of a thoughtful scarf – and
    really I just wanted to check,
If it will be pondering life whilst it hangs round my
    neck?

DIAMENDS

Diamonds are a girls best friend,
Is this an accurate message to send?
Most jewel thieves are actually men,
They steal the sparklies again and again.
Perhaps it's the glint that catches their eye,
An impulse takes over as they pass by.
Is it simply that ladies have more respect?
For us those stones have a special effect.
Rather than stealing them from other homes,
We covet them and put them up high on thrones,
They adorn our fingers and necks and ears,
A shiny keepsake that lasts for years.
You never know perhaps these thieving men,
Just want to sparkle now and again.

SNAILS FOR BRAINS

Have you ever thought like a snail?
To these simple creatures all hail,
You see they make decisions very well,
In that their brains never swell –
With the effort because they –
Only use a few brain cells in a day.

So all robots are taking tips,
Yes they may be held together by clips,
But they need help from these slimy creatures,
Who only use two brain cells – among other top
    snail features.
So next time you over-think what to have for lunch,
Feel pity for the victim of your pavement crunch.